Pau[l] M…

NOW SLE… …HE CRIMSON PETAL

for SATB divisi chorus unaccompanied

NOVELLO

Now Sleeps the Crimson Petal

Four Madrigals on Rose Texts for SATB (with divisi)

PAUL MEALOR

Commissioned by John Armitage Memorial
and first performed by the joint choirs of the University of St Andrews Chapel Choir,
University of Aberdeen Chamber Choir and the Edinburgh University Chamber Choir
Conducted by Michael Bawtree
October 28th, 29th & 31st 2010

No. I: Now sleeps the crimson petal (Tennyson)

To Edward & Sarah Armitage with admiration and thanks

*This may be sung by second sopranos only, or, the altos may be divided here instead

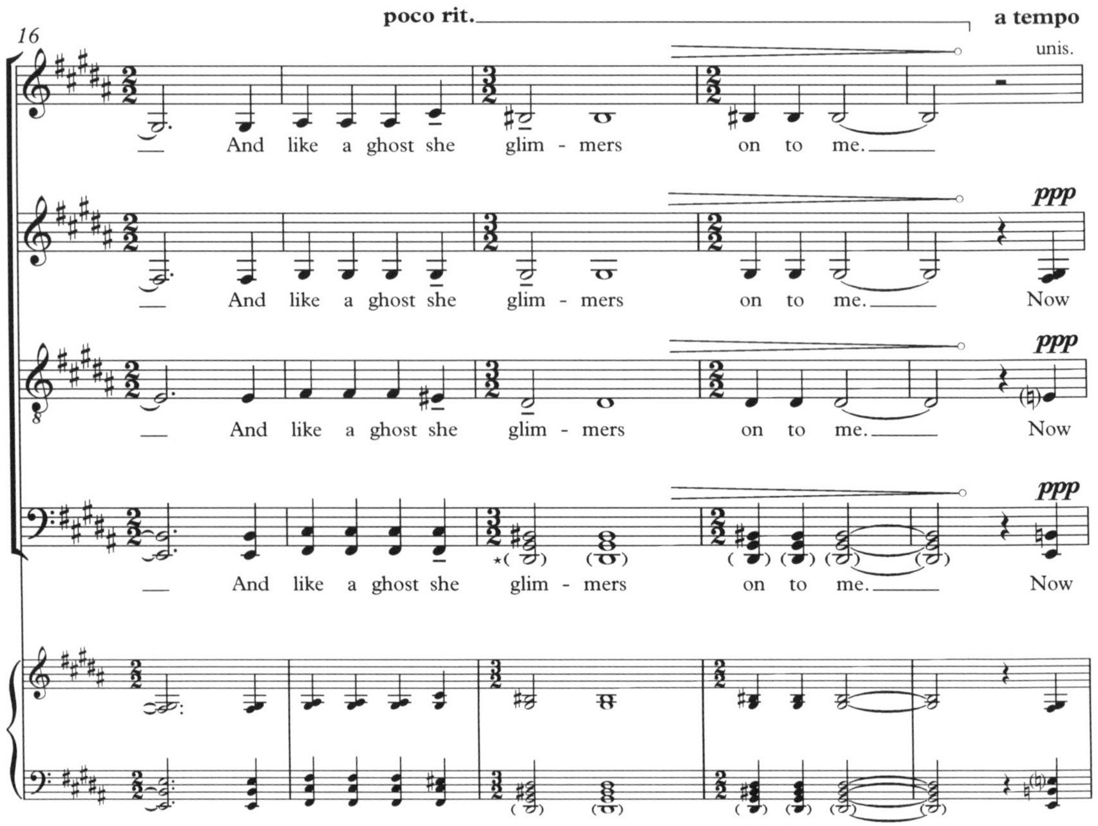

* Bracketed notes are optional divisi.

26
rit.
a tempo
mf
o - pen un - to me. Now
o - pen un - to me. Now
o - pen un - to me.
o - pen un - to me.
B
30
poco rit.
a tempo
f
folds the li - ly all her sweet - ness up, And slips in - to the bo-som
folds the li - ly all her sweet - ness up, And slips in - to the bo-som
mf
Now folds the li - ly all her sweet - ness up, And slips in - to the bo-som
Now folds the li - ly all her sweet-ness up, And slips in - to the bo-som

*This may be sung by second sopranos only, or, the Altos may be divided here instead

rall.
= c. 48
mancando
45
unis.
ppp
in
me
Now
ppp
in
me
Now
in
me
in
me
C
49
sleeps the crim-son pe - tal
sleeps the crim-son pe - tal
ppp
now the white.
ppp
now the white.

Selected choral music by

PAUL MEALOR

Ave Maria
SATB
NOV292765

Ave Maris Stella
SATB
NOV292875

Beata es, Virgo Maria
SATB
NOV292776

Locus iste
SATB
NOV292831

Lux Benigna
SSAAA and piano
NOV292787

Now Sleeps the Crimson Petal
Four madrigals for SATB divisi NOV292710;
I: Now sleeps the crimson petal NOV292721;
II: Lady, when I behold the roses sprouting NOV292732;
III: Upon a bank with roses set about NOV292743;
IV: A Spotless Rose NOV292754

O Sanctissima Maria
SATB NOV292798;
TTBB NOV292809

O vos omnes
SATB divisi and tubular bells
NOV292842

Sanctuary Haunts
SATB
NOV292820

She walks in beauty
SSAATTBB
NOV162074

Stabat Mater
Solo soprano, SATB divisi, harp (or piano) and strings
Full score NOV292864;
Vocal score NOV292853

Ubi caritas
SATB divisi NOV200937;
Pack of ten NOV200937-10;
Pack of twenty-five NOV200937-25

Wherever you are
SSA and piano NOV201146;
SATB and piano NOV292886;
TTBB and piano NOV292897
All available in packs of ten (-10) or twenty-five (-25)

SSA, piano, percussion and strings
Full score NOV201135

Novello Publishing Limited
part of the Music Sales Group
14/15 Berners Street
London W1T 3LJ

Exclusive distributors:
Music Sales Ltd
Newmarket Road
Bury St Edmunds
Suffolk, IP33 3YB

www.chesternovello.com

Order No. NOV292721

ISBN 978-1-78038-497-9

Paul Mealor NOW SLEEPS THE CRIMSON PETAL for SATB divisi chorus unaccompanied NOVELLO